Funny
(But True)
Golf
Anecdotes

Funny
(But True)
Golf
Anecdotes

Dick Crouser

Meadowbrook Press
Distributed by Simon & Schuster
New York

Library of Congress Cataloging-in-Publication Data
Crouser, Dick.
Golf's funniest anecdotes / by Dick Crouser.
          p.   cm.
ISBN 978-0-88166-577-2 (Meadowbrook)
ISBN 978-1-4516-7076-9 (Simon & Schuster)
1. Golf—Humor. 2. Golf—Anecdotes. I. Title.
GV967 .C74 2001
796.352—dc21   00-051140

Managing Editor: Christine Zuchora-Walske
Copyeditors: Joseph Gredler and Alicia Ester
Proofreaders: Angela Wiechmann and Alicia Ester
Coordinating Editors: Megan McGinnis and Bruce Lansky
Creative Director: Tamara JM Peterson
Production Manager: Paul Woods
Cover Photo: Cameramannz
Illustrations: Jack Johnson
Researchers: Bruce Lansky, and Phil Theibert

© 2001, 2012 by Dick Crouser

Published by Meadowbrook Press
6110 Blue Circle Drive, Suite 237, Minnetonka, MN 55343

www.meadowbrookpress.com

BOOK TRADE DISTRIBUTION by
Simon & Schuster, a division of Simon and Schuster, Inc.
1230 Avenue of the Americas, New York, NY 10020

16 15 14 13 12   10 9 8 7 6 5 4 3 2

Printed in the United States of America

Dedication

For Dan, Mike, Jenny, and Pete, four fine folks without whom I wouldn't be a father.

Acknowledgments

We would like to thank the individuals who served on reading panels for this project:

Phil Theibert, Leo Verrett, Jim Rallis, George Winsor, Thomas Courage, Trevor Lloyd, Ned Pastor, Tim Tocher, Dr. Paul Driscoll, Bob Zahn, Ron Tracy, Norman Meltzer, John Foote, Gib Poiry, F. Blaine Dickson, Frank Gredler, Marvin Wallace, Linda Cave, Ron Zuchora-Walske, Dave Waldorf, Bruce Huffaker, Patrick Bowyer

Introduction

When a fella can combine two of his favorite things and actually get paid for it, well, it just doesn't get any better than that. I'm kicked back in a lounge chair, surrounded by books and magazines, in search of the snappiest punch lines, the funniest put-downs, and the greatest comeback lines from the wonderful world of golf.

The missus, passing through and noticing that I seem to be enjoying myself rather excessively, interrupts, "What are you doing and why aren't you mowing the lawn?" "Sorry, dear," I reply solemnly, "I'm working."

Humor and golf. A delightful pair. A natural pair. Because with all its frustrations, tensions, absurdities, and cruel twists of fate, golf provides a rich and fertile field for humor.

Can any sport match it for fun and games? For fun and gamesmanship?

Well…baseball…maybe.

Baseball! Now, there's a thought.

Excuse me, won't you? I have work to do.

Dick Crouser

The Funniest Thing Feherty Ever Saw

Years ago TV golf analyst David Feherty was playing in a Pro-Am tournament in Ireland, where he was teamed up with an amateur whose ball had landed on a steep incline. Apparently the cold Irish weather had turned the ground hard as a rock, so when the amateur topped his next shot, it bounced straight back up and hit him in a most painful and embarrassing spot. The blow "doubled him up for five minutes" while Feherty and the other team were doubled up too—not from pain, but from laughter.

A Man of Few Words?

Bantam Ben Hogan was called "The Iceman" both for his coolness under fire and for his aversion to small talk during a match. But Jimmy Demaret was quick to defend his old partner: "Hogan not very chatty? Nonsense," he said. "He'd speak to me on almost every green. He'd say, 'You're away.'"

Scottish Golf Etiquette

Working the British Open at Muirfield one year, broadcaster Ray Scott tried to make a quick visit to a nearby porta-potty. The line was long, but an elderly Scotsman standing ahead of Ray noticed him nervously checking his watch. With a gracious bow, the man said, "Would ye care to play through, laddie?"

Irish Golf Etiquette

What will those rascally Irish do next? A friend who returned recently from a golfing trip to Ireland reported seeing a notice posted outside the clubhouse of a course he played. It read, "Trousers are now allowed to be worn by ladies on the course, but they must be removed before entering the clubhouse."

Dicky Pride's Office

Dicky Pride struck a blow for the anti-cell phone movement at the 1999 Honda Classic at Coral Springs, Florida. While lining up a putt, his concentration was broken by a spectator's phone ringing just beyond the gallery ropes. Pride said, "Excuse me, sir, I'm working here. If you have to work, would you please go to your office?"

Pro-Am Strategy

Los Angeles Times sportswriter Jim Murray was a slightly better writer than golfer. Okay, a lot better. He was once paired with pro Donna Caponi in an alternate-shot match, and he sorely tested her patience. She hit a booming tee shot; he scuffed one into the woods. She hit out of the woods onto the green; he putted off the green into the water. After several holes like this, she hit a big drive that stopped just in front of a water hazard. "What should I do here?" he asked. "Whiff it," she said.

A Tough Golf Course

Robert Trent Jones was never the pro golfer's favorite architect, because many felt that Jones had something against a golfer being able to shoot par. Jimmy Demaret, one of Jones's severest critics, ran into him once and said, "Saw a course you'd really like the other day, Trent. On the first tee, you take a penalty drop."

An Asterisk in the Record Books

The incredible success with which Tiger Woods began his professional career prompted Brad Faxon to suggest that a notation be added to the record books. "If you win a tournament and Tiger didn't play in it," said Faxon, "there should be an asterisk next to your name."

Palmer's Punch Line

Bob Hope played with many great golfers over the years and, presumably, picked up a fair amount of free advice along the way. In return, he may have occasionally loaned his writers to some of the pros. Hope once asked Arnold Palmer to comment on his new swing, and Arnie replied, "I've seen better swings on a condemned playground."

Bubba's Bid to Get on Ellen's Show

In January 2010, Bubba Watson shot a video at the house he was renting during the Bob Hope Classic, hoping it would get him invited on *The Ellen DeGeneres Show*. It featured a trick shot through a door, over a pool, and into a red bucket decorated with balloons. After sinking the shot into the bucket, he celebrated by sliding into the pool fully dressed, and made Ellen an offer he hoped she couldn't refuse: "I can show you this trick shot and you can teach me how to dance." A month later, he got his wish and appeared on her show, and Ellen kept up her end of the bargain. The next time Bubba chips in over a water hazard, he'll have some new Hollywood dance moves to show off.

What Do You Tip a Caddie?

Old-time comedian Jimmy Durante decided he'd like to try golf, so he took a couple of lessons and got a few buddies to join him on his first full round. It was a disaster. Jimmy barely broke 200. He wanted to do the right thing when the round ended, so he asked one of the guys what he should give the caddie. "Your clubs," the man answered.

One Long Winning Streak

Jack Nicklaus got off to a somewhat shaky start in the 1991 Tradition. After the first two rounds, he found himself 12 strokes behind the leader. But then he regained his edge and fired rounds of 66 and 67 to win the tournament and the sizeable first-place check. Afterward, someone asked Frank Beard if he thought Nicklaus was really that good. "No," Beard replied, "he's been on a thirty-year lucky streak."

Ken Venturi in Disguise

Ken Venturi was having lunch at Winged Foot with member Jack Whitaker, and they decided to play a round. Since Venturi had neither clubs nor clothes, Whitaker borrowed some clubs and found him a tattered sweater and a ratty old hat. On the ninth fairway, Venturi was 2 under and had just hit a spectacular shot for an easy eagle putt. His caddie looked at him wide-eyed and said, "I don't know who you are, mister, but if you come back here tomorrow dressed like that, we can make a lotta money."

Success with a 1-Iron

Many are the horror stories that have grown up around the infamous 1-iron. Sportswriter Jim Murray was definitely not a fan of the club. "The only time I ever used a 1-iron successfully was to kill a tarantula," said Murray, "and even then it took me seven strokes to do it."

Kevin Na's Worst-Hole Record

At the 2011 Valero Texas Open, Korean golfer Kevin Na established a PGA record for the worst score ever on a par-4 hole: 16 strokes. While walking to the tenth tee with his caddie, Na complained about all the rocks he hit while trying to blast the ball out of the woods. After letting Na vent his frustration, the caddie offered Na some sound advice: "Next time I say 'Let's go back to the tee'—let's go back to the tee!"

An Easy Choice

A nasty part of the campaign against Dan Quayle when he was running for vice-president in 1988 was a bogus story put forth by a woman who claimed she'd had a rendezvous with Quayle during a one-day golf trip he'd taken. It was quickly and confidently squelched by Marilyn Quayle, who said, "Anyone who knows Dan knows that given the choice between golf and sex, he'd take golf every time." The story died immediately.

Elaine Johnson's Awkward Lie

One of golf's most difficult decisions is whether to try a shot from an awkward lie or to take a drop and the penalty that goes with it. Elaine Johnson's decision was easy. After she sliced a shot into a nearby tree, the ball bounced back and lodged in her halter top. "I'll take the penalty," she said. "I absolutely refuse to play it where it lies."

The Clothes Make the Man

Bob Hope's golf game was never good enough for him to quit his day job, but he kept plugging away. After one miserable round, however, he was especially discouraged. "I'd give up the game," he said, "if I didn't have so many sweaters."

Slash and Burn

Arnold Palmer's slash-and-burn approach became his trademark early on and, until he mellowed a bit, got him into a lot of trouble. In one West Coast tournament, he had missed a green badly. As he was studying the unpleasant options, he noticed sportswriter Jim Murray in the gallery. "What would Hogan do in a spot like this, Jim?" he asked. "Hogan wouldn't be in a spot like that," said Murray.

Tiger Woods Vs. Michael Jordan

How do Tiger Woods and Michael Jordan handicap each other when they go head-to-head in golf or basketball? According to Jordan, ten seems to be the operative number. Ten strokes for Jordan sounds about right, but should he give Tiger ten points at hoops? "I give him ten points and beat him in a game to eleven," explains Jordan, "and I give him the ball to start out."

What's the Address?

Before there was John Daly and Tiger Woods, there was Jim Dent, a guy who could crush the ball off the tee. However, big hitters tend to be a bit erratic now and then. As Dent put it, "Sure I can airmail the ball, but sometimes I have the wrong address on it."

How Bad Was That Swing?

Most average golfers' swing problems will seem pretty minor if they have a chance to watch a tournament of blind players. There they'll see true resolve and dedication—and a bit of humor, too. Once, blind golfer Charlie Boswell was standing near a tee box while an opponent was hitting. After the swing, Boswell shook his head and muttered, "Worst swing I've ever heard!"

Lee Trevino's History Lesson

Lee Trevino has always had a good word to say about everyone, even historical figures. Lee once remarked, "Columbus went around the world in 1492. That isn't a lot of strokes when you consider the course."

Putting for Dough

Bob Hope was playing a round with film mogul Sam Goldwyn when Sam missed a short putt and, in a rage, threw the putter away. On the way to the next hole, Hope picked up the offending putter and put it in his bag while Goldwyn wasn't looking. Two holes later, Hope used the reclaimed putter to drain a long one. "Great shot," said Goldwyn. "Let me see that club." He looked it over and said, "I like this putter. I'll give you fifty bucks for it." "Done," said Hope.

A Stupid Choice

Near the end of one of his high-volume, temperamental, club-throwing rounds, "Terrible" Tommy Bolt asked his caddie to recommend a club for a 155-yard shot. "I'd say either a 3-iron or a wedge, sir," said the caddie. "A 3-iron or a wedge?" said Bolt. "What kind of stupid choice is that?" "Those are the only clubs you have left, sir," said the caddie.

Brent Geiberger's 59

Does Brent Geiberger ever get tired of hearing about his father, Al, becoming the first pro to shoot a 59 in a PGA event? Well, when Brent won the 1999 Greater Hartford Open, he at least put a new spin on the matter. "I shoot 59 every time I play," he said. "Of course, at that point I usually have a few holes left."

Phil's Bad Luck Putt

Putting for a birdie on the second hole at the 2010 Masters, Phil Mickelson surveyed the steep 6-foot downhill putt, took his backswing, hit the ball, and watched it roll over a small brown object that hadn't been on the green before he'd started his swing. Phil's ball rolled over the tiny "speed bump," slowed down, and abruptly changed direction—to the left of the hole. The unlucky Mickelson missed his birdie chance and had to settle for a par. Several replays by the amazed TV crew showed that what could have been the stem of a leaf, a twig, a worm, or a piece of pretzel had dropped from the sky. Mickelson was tied with Lee Westwood for the lead at the time, but eventually recovered from his "bad luck putt" and won.

The Power of Suggestion

Talk about the power of suggestion. John F. Kennedy was playing a round at Seminole with its chairman, Chris Dunphy. On the first green, Kennedy faced a 3-footer and said, "Is this good, Chris?" Dunphy replied, "Oh, I don't know, why don't you putt that one." Kennedy responded, "Oh, by the way, I can't dawdle. I have a meeting with the head of the IRS in a few hours." Dunphy replied, "The putt's good, Jack."

A Long Day on the Golf Course

"Home Run King" Hank Aaron found it a lot easier to hit a fastball thrown at 95 mph than to hit a stationary golf ball straight. He was once quoted as saying, "It took me seventeen years to get three thousand hits in baseball. I did it in one afternoon on the golf course."

The Only Game Babe Didn't Play

Babe Didrikson Zaharias is considered by many to be the best female athlete of all time. She set world records at the Olympics, starred in softball, and won seventeen tournaments in a row on the women's pro golf tour. Writer Paul Gallico once asked Babe if there were any games she didn't play as a kid. "Yes," she said, "dolls I didn't play."

The Secret of His Longevity

After Mike Mazzeo had caddied for Fuzzy Zoeller for more than fifteen years, he was asked to reveal the secret of his longevity in an occupation noted for its rapid turnover. Was it his club-selection skills, his knowledge of courses, his rock-steady demeanor under pressure? "No," said Mazzeo. "After twenty years, I know too much. He's afraid to fire me."

Consistency Off the Tee

Jackie Burke was a successful pro golfer back in the thirties, but he never had much luck against the immortal Byron Nelson. Burke was especially frustrated by Nelson's consistency off the tee. "The only time Byron Nelson ever left the fairway," said Burke, "was to go pee in the woods."

Henrik Stenson's Striptease

Few Americans had heard of Swedish golfer Henrik Stenson before 2009, but his obscurity ended when he was shown on the news playing a shot out of deep mud wearing only his skivvies and a golf glove. He knocked the ball out of the muck, dressed, and finished the hole with a bogey. Stenson justified his striptease by claiming it had saved him a stroke, and added, "I don't think I scared too many spectators off the course..."

Jack Nicklaus, Oenologist

One of the interests Jack Nicklaus developed after conquering golf was wine. Nicklaus and writer Dick Taylor were once seated together at a PGA dinner, when Taylor decided to test Nicklaus's knowledge of the subject. As several bottles of fine wine wrapped in linen were delivered to their table, Taylor challenged Nicklaus to identify each one sight unseen. Nicklaus swirled and tasted—and identified each precisely. Later, Taylor mentioned to Deane Beman how impressed he had been with Nicklaus's skills. "He should have known them all," said Beman. "He's the one who picked them for the dinner."

A Cure for Insomnia

David Feherty remembers some medical advice that didn't work for his golfing father, William, back in Ireland's County Down. A physician tried to cure the elder Feherty's insomnia by encouraging him to play an imaginary round of golf in his head while lying in bed. Reporting back to the doctor, William said, "I played great until the third tee shot, which I sliced into the woods. Then I was awake all night looking for the ball."

Faldo's Pricey Present

Nick Faldo had just won the biggest purse of his life—a cool $1 million—and was feeling generous when he asked his wife if there were anything she'd like to have. "A divorce," she said. "I wasn't thinking of anything quite that expensive," Faldo replied.

The Power of Positive Thinking

In his prime, Arnold Palmer's positive, go-for-it style endeared him to a whole generation of golf fans. He dripped with confidence. Gene Littler was especially impressed with Palmer's attitude on the greens. "I'm always surprised when one of my putts drops," Littler said, "but it never occurs to Arnold that his ball won't go in the hole."

Lily Tomlin on Gravity

Emmy, Grammy, and Tony Award-winner Lily Tomlin has spent some time on the golf course, but she hasn't won any awards there. Her frustrations are summed up by this comment about gravity: "What goes up must come down. But don't expect it to come down where you can find it.

Listen to Your Mother

Basketball great Bill Russell wasn't always the avid golfer he became once his remarkable career with the Celtics ended. "When I was growing up, my mother wouldn't let me near a golf course," said Russell. "She didn't think golfers were very nice people. And now that I play every day, I realize she was right."

Nothing Left to Learn

Claude Harmon's son Dick never matched his dad's exploits on the tour, but Dick became a great teacher of the game. Lanny Wadkins once came to Houston for a session with Dick at a time when Claude was also in town, and the three of them played a round. At one point, Lanny hit a tremendous downhill-lie 3-wood about 2 feet from the pin on a guarded green. "Tell me, son," Claude said to Dick, "what is it you plan to teach this young man?"

Willie Nelson's Golf Course

At last, the answer to a duffer's problems: Buy your own golf course. When asked what par was for the course he had just bought, singer Willie Nelson said, "Anything I want it to be. This hole right here, for example, is a par-47," said Nelson, "and yesterday I birdied the sucker."

The Power of Prayer

Evangelist Billy Graham, who has counseled and prayed with every American president from Harry Truman to Barack Obama, could talk on the subject of prayer for hours, but when asked whether praying had helped his golf game, he would respond, "The Lord answers my prayers everywhere except on the course."

Par Golf Isn't Boring

Doesn't it get boring for the pro golfer to play every hole in regulation? Drive down the middle, hit the green, and then two-putt. Why not take a few chances and have some fun? Lee Trevino tells us why not: "There are two things that are not long for this world," he says. "Dogs who chase cars and golfers who chip for pars."

Steep Green

What's so tough about Pennsylvania's Oakmont Country Club course? Well, the greens, for one thing. Some say that putting there is like trying to stop a ball halfway down a flight of marble steps. Sam Snead claimed that he once marked a ball on an Oakmont green and the marker slid downhill.

Hagen's Confidence

The legendary Walter Hagen was as famous for his late-night barroom adventures as he was for his exploits on the golf course. And no one ever accused him of being short on self-confidence. On one occasion, it was past midnight on the eve of a big match, and a concerned bartender tried to convince Hagen to get some shuteye. "Your opponent's been in bed for hours," the bartender said. "Young man," said Hagen, "he may have retired, but he knows whom he's playing tomorrow, and you may be sure he hasn't slept a wink."

Oh, What A Beautiful Day

David Feherty, a fine golfer in his own right, has also become famous as a witty golf analyst. After two days of fog at the PGA Championship at Whistling Straits, the sun finally came out, prompting Feherty to note, "Gorgeous. There's only one way you can ruin a day like this, and that's to play golf."

Club-Throwing Expertise

Forget about all the tournaments Tommy Bolt has won and all the money he's taken home; his name will forever be associated with club throwing. And as the ultimate authority on the subject, he frequently dispenses advice. For example, "Always throw the club forward so you can pick it up on your way down the fairway." Jimmy Demaret once described Bolt's credentials on the subject: "Tommy Bolt's putter has had more air time than Lindbergh."

When Bob Costas Interviewed Paul Goydos

There are very few questions for which Paul Goydos doesn't have a funny response. During the 2008 Players Championship Tournament, he even ruffled NBC's unflappable Bob Costas a couple of times. Costas: "Why do you wear your shirts buttoned to the top on a 90-degree day?" Goydos: "Because I don't have any shoulders, and this is the way the shirt stays on." Costas: "Have you ever held the 54-hole lead?" Goydos: "No, but I've only been out on tour for sixteen years."

Jack's Physics Lesson

Jack Nicklaus's skills and his performances over the years are the stuff of legends. But it would seem he hasn't received enough credit for his teaching ability and his tips for playing the game. When explaining why one should tee the ball high, for example, Nicklaus says, "Years of experience have shown me that air offers less resistance than dirt."

Secret Scores

Show biz people have traditionally loved the game of golf. Jack Lemmon, Dean Martin, Michael Douglas, to name just a few. And they've enjoyed hanging around the big hitters at tournaments. But many Hollywood stars have been sensitive about revealing their scores. Old-time comedian Joe E. Lewis neatly avoided the subject when he said, "I usually play in the low 80s. If it's any warmer than that, I don't go out."

Lightning Won't Strike Lee Again

Lee Trevino has been hit by lightning on the golf course and has not enjoyed the experience. So he's settled on a policy of rapidly fleeing the course when it starts to storm. "When God wants to play through, I let him play through," he says.

Denser than Water

Craig Stadler doesn't throw his clubs as often or as far as Tommy Bolt, but his style is good and his range is pretty decent. Once, after watching Stadler hole out on 18, a friend asked him why he was using a new putter. "Because my old one didn't float," Stadler replied.

The High Cost of Winning

Back in the days when tournament purses were a bit more modest than they are today, Ben Hogan demonstrated his practical side. He initiated the custom of the Masters winner hosting the following year's Champions Dinner. But after winning one year, Hogan seemed to have a change of heart. "When I discovered that the cost of the dinner was more than the prize money," he said, "I finished second four times."

How Slow Is Sakura Yokomine?

LPGA star Christina Kim has never been known for keeping her opinions to herself. After learning she wouldn't have to play behind Japanese player Sakura Yokomine during the final round of the U.S. Women's Open, Kim said, "Phew. I'm glad… She's slower than trying to bake a pie with a lighter."

Palmer's Famous 11

It was the third round of the Los Angeles Open, and Arnold Palmer needed only a par on 18 to give him a 69 and the lead. But he hit his second shot out-of-bounds. Then he hit another OB. And another. He finally limped in with a horrendous 12. "How in the world could you make a 12?" a reporter asked Arnie. "I missed a 20-footer for my 11," said Palmer.

Who Could Forget?

Despite their numerous heroics, athletes are sometimes remembered for the one glaring mistake they made: Bill Buckner for the World Series grounder that went through his legs; Chris Webber for the ill-fated time-out in the NCAA finals; Doug Sanders for the 2-foot putt that would have won him the British Open in 1970. Does Sanders still think about that putt after all these years? "Oh, I sometimes go as long as four or five minutes without thinking about it," he says.

Parnevik's Peculiar Style

If eccentric Scandinavian golfer Jesper Parnevik thinks of himself as a fashion setter, he should think again. His bill-turned-up baseball cap trademark has never quite caught on here in America. When describing Jesper's peculiar style, sportswriter Dan Jenkins said, "Parnevik always looks like the last guy to climb out of the clown car at the circus."

When Crenshaw Met Penick

Ben Crenshaw was eight years old the first time he came to Harvey Penick for a lesson. Harvey cut down a 7-iron and asked Ben to hit a ball to a green about 75 yards away. He did. "Good," said Harvey, "now take this putter and go up and putt the ball into the hole." "Why didn't you tell me to do that on the first shot?" asked Ben.

The Golfing Dentist

Cary Middlecoff, the "golfing dentist" and one of the top players of the forties and fifties, was noted for his annoyingly slow play. Writer Dan Jenkins claims that Middlecoff finally gave up dentistry because none of his patients could hold their mouths open that long.

Gleason's Handicap

Most golfers have two handicaps: the numerical one and the physical one. For comedian Jackie Gleason, the physical one was quite obviously his waistline. "When I put the ball where I can see it, I can't hit it," he said. "And when I put it where I can hit it, I can't see it."

Mystery Golfer

Three friends were teeing off at St. Andrews when the starter told them to wait for a fourth player they didn't know. Once introduced, the fourth player asked them their handicaps. They told him, and the fourth player, who was right handed, said, "Okay, I'll get my left-handed clubs." Using those, he proceeded to shoot a 3 over par 75. Who was the fourth player? Spaniard Seve Ballesteros, a brilliant golfer who won three Open Championships, two Masters, and eighty-two other titles.

How Long Are John Daly's Drives?

When John Daly first appeared on the tour, those in the golfing world tried to find ways to describe his booming drives. Gay Brewer said, "I can't even point that far." Fuzzy Zoeller chipped in, "By the time we walk up to his drive, my clothes have gone out of style." And writer Bob Verdi said, "He's longer than Couples or Norman. He's longer than Tolstoy!"

The Woman Has a Point

Tom Lehman has learned that every round of golf teaches you something, even in a mixed, alternate-shot tournament. At the first hole, Tom hit his tee shot about 275 yards. His wife, Melissa, shanked the ball into the rough. Tom then hit out of the rough to within 10 feet of the pin, only to have Melissa send her putt 25 feet past the cup. After Tom sank the comebacker, he suggested to her that she'd have to do a little better if they were to contend. She responded, "Hey, you took three shots. I took only two!"

Fewer Purses and Smaller Galleries

Near the end of Gene Littler's career, his dwindling game resulted in fewer purses and smaller galleries. Following one round, however, he came into the players' lounge with a huge smile and said, "Well, I guess I've still got the old charisma. Had a huge gallery out there today." Someone asked who his partner was. "Palmer," he said offhandedly.

Chi Chi's Take on Tennis

Chi Chi Rodriguez's first love is, of course, golf. It's not that he hasn't tried other sports. He's just found them wanting. Take tennis, for example. "Getting two serves is unfair," says Chi Chi. "The guy can wind up and blast one at you, and if he misses, he gets a mulligan."

Another Club-Thrower Heard From

U.S. Open runner-up Paul Azinger was less famous for club-throwing than "Terrible" Tommy Bolt, but Azinger never kept that aspect of his game a secret. He once explained his distaste for video golf by quipping, "I don't enjoy playing video golf because there's nothing to throw."

Practice Makes Perfect?

Playing in the first half of the twentieth century, Walter Hagen won eleven major tournaments to rank third, all time, behind Jack Nicklaus and Tiger Woods. But unlike Nicklaus and Woods, he didn't believe in practice, remarking "What a shame to waste all those great shots on the practice tee." Gary Player, who won nine majors, disagreed: "The more I play," he said, "the luckier I get."

Snead's Dirty Trick

Sam Snead was playing a practice round at Augusta National with the much younger Bobby Cole (with a few bucks riding on the match, of course). Reaching the tee at the dogleg-left par-5, Snead said, "You know Bobby, when I was your age, I'd drive the ball right over those trees at the corner." Feeling challenged, Bobby hit a big drive right *into* the big trees. Snead said, "Of course, when I was your age, those trees were only ten feet high."

When Cristie Kerr Kissed the Golf Trophy

When Cristie Kerr won the LPGA Longs Drugs Challenge in 2002, she was happy to plant a kiss on her new trophy for photographers. But she couldn't have been very pleased when she saw the photo printed in newspapers the next day— the cylindrical glass object looked more like a bachelorette party gag gift than a golf trophy.

Maltbie's Last-Round Comeback

The thrill and drama of the last-round comeback has made tournament golf a huge spectator draw. Palmer, Nicklaus, Woods, Love, Faldo—they've all done it. Roger Maltbie has, too, although he didn't seem to possess the supreme confidence golf miracles normally require. Ten strokes back entering the last round of an Andy Williams tourney, he was asked what he'd have to shoot to win. "The rest of the field," he said.

Unlucky in Love

Lee Trevino was much luckier in golf than he was in love. "You can make a lot of money in this game," he said. "Just ask my ex-wives. Both of them are so rich that neither of their husbands work."

Aaron Baddeley's Nickname

Australian golfer Aaron Baddeley knows his reputation for being out of step with fashion is deserved. Says Baddeley, "In the locker room at Bay Hill, Tiger Woods saw my light-green pants and called out, 'Man you've got guts!'" Bad as his fashion sense may be, Baddeley has a great sense of humor. "I've got a new nickname on tour: 'Dresses'—as in 'Dresses Baddeley'!"

Talk About Erratic Golfers

As a substantial number of wounded spectators can verify, some of our twentieth-century presidents have reputations for hitting the golf ball erratically. At the 1995 Bob Hope Classic, as a foursome that included Gerald Ford, George Bush, and Bill Clinton was getting ready to hit from the first tee, Barbara Bush was heard to say, "As if we don't have enough violence on television."

Following Orders

Tommy Bolt was in an ugly mood one day, and on the first tee he told his caddie he didn't want to hear a single word from him. Late in the round, Bolt found himself with a difficult shot and asked the caddie what he thought about a 5-iron. Following Bolt's instructions, the caddie said nothing. Bolt proceeded to hit a great shot and said, "Well, what do you think of that?" Breaking his silence at last, the caddie said, "That wasn't your ball, Mr. Bolt."

No Sympathy for Nicklaus

Even the greatest golfer (read: Nicklaus) has his frustrations. Jack was finishing a round at the Tournament of Champions in Las Vegas. But not happily. He had missed an eagle putt on 18 and stormed off the green muttering, "No matter how I try, I can't break 64 on this course!" A nearby writer sympathized: "What a terrible thing to have to go through life with…"

Crenshaw's Concentration Problem

Ben Crenshaw has kept improving through the years, but his biggest problem has been periodic lapses in concentration. At one point during one of his more successful periods, a reporter asked him how far he thought he was from being ranked among the best. "About five inches," said Ben. "The distance between my ears."

The Break-Up

When a player and caddie are together for several years, the bond between them can seem unbreakable. But during the 1995 Tournament Players Championship, caddie Mike Mazzeo found that his twenty-year relationship with Fuzzy Zoeller was on shaky ground. Mike had kept Fuzzy waiting on the first tee, claiming he was on a work slowdown because he hadn't been making much money of late. "You're making less now," said Zoeller as he fired him.

Trevino's Attention Deficit

Lee Trevino claims that when he first came on the tour, he smiled and laughed and told jokes, and no one paid any attention to him. "Then, in 1968, I won the U.S. Open," he says. "I told the same jokes, did the same routines, and everybody laughed."

Tony Lema, Mind Reader

The player with the most glamorous nickname in the fifties and sixties was "Champagne" Tony Lema. In private, he probably didn't imbibe enough of the bubbly to warrant the name, but he still enjoyed the notoriety. Once, when asked by a reporter to reveal how much he drank, Tony said, "Not as much as you do." "How do you know that?" asked the man. "Because only a drunk would ask the question," said Lema.

When Women Were Banned

Like a number of staid old clubs, the Royal St. George's at Sandwich, England, banned women from the course for many years. This policy became a problem when the Cambridge University team came to Royal St. George's for their annual match, and it was discovered that Miss Fiona MacDonald was on the Cambridge roster. Proving once again why "there'll always be an England," the Royal St. George's committee sat down over brandy and cigars and hammered out a solution: They declared MacDonald an honorary man.

Changing the Rules on Ernie at the U.S. Open

In the final round of the 1994 U.S. Open, Ernie Els hit his first shot into four inches of shag. U.S. Golf Association official Trey Holland ruled that a mobile TV crane had blocked his line of vision to the green and gave Els a free drop and an improved lie. This helped Els into a three-way playoff—where he found himself in the same rough (off the first tee). Holland changed his mind about the crane, deciding that he had made a mistake—and Els had to play the shot over the lowered crane. Despite the fluctuating official decrees, Els still managed to win the Open.

Sudden Death

One year, Billy Joe Patton was on the second hole of a sudden-death playoff in the North and South Amateur at Pinehurst. His opponent was on in two, but Billy Joe's second shot was buried under the lip of a fairway bunker. As he struggled for some footing for an impossible shot, a car stopped on the greenside road and a man yelled, "Anybody know where I can get a room?" "If you wait a couple of minutes," said Billy Joe, "you can probably have mine."

Where's the Drop?

Playing in the 1964 Crosby Clambake, Arnold Palmer had a problem. Coming up the 17th fairway, he had hit a shot down the cliff and into the Pacific Ocean. Someone asked TV commentator Jimmy Demaret what choices Palmer had for his next shot. "I don't know," said Demaret. "His nearest drop from there would be Honolulu."

The Comeback Kid

Ken Venturi's life was at its lowest ebb in 1964. His game, his marriage, and his finances were all in shambles, and he was ready to quit the tour. Then, in one of professional sports' most dramatic comebacks, he won the U.S. Open and his career flourished again. By 1974, he was playing only part-time and was out of contention at the U.S. Open at Winged Foot. Struggling up one of the final fairways, he heard a man in the gallery say, "If I were him, I'd quit." Venturi was cheered to hear the man's companion say, "Yeah, and if you were him you'd have quit ten years ago, too."

Phil Mickelson's Rumored Gambling Loss

In April 2008, an online edition of *Golfweek* seemed to fan the flames of a rumor that Phil Mickelson had lost big bucks betting against three unnamed golfers on a practice round in Augusta. Mickelson was said to be so confident in his game, he escalated the stakes from $1 a game to six figures. But according to the story, his luck turned against him and by the time he reached the clubhouse he had allegedly lost $200,000. When curious readers wrote in to see if the *Golfweek* story was true, editor Jeff Babineau replied that it wasn't, and mentioned the date it had been posted: April 1.

Hogan's Putting Advice

Ben Hogan was never much for giving free advice. He once had a playing partner who complained constantly about his putting, especially his long approach putts. Finally, the man asked Hogan if he had any tips. "Did you ever think about hitting them closer to the hole?" Ben said.

No Talent Required

We know that Jimmy Demaret was a great golfer. So we can probably assume he didn't have himself in mind when he said, "Golf and sex are the only things you can enjoy without being good at them."

Greg Norman's Missed Opportunity

Byron Nelson is one of the greatest golfers of all time, but he's also a realist. Greg Norman won the Byron Nelson Award in 1995, and as Nelson was handing him the trophy, Norman said, "Byron, I'm just sorry that you and I never had a chance to compete against one another." "I'm not," said Nelson.

Daly's Mulligan

At the 1993 Houston Open, a longest-drive contest was held between John Daly and Jim Dent with these rules: you could take two swings, but if you chose to hit the second ball, that's the one that counted. Dent hit his first ball 318 yards and settled for that. Daly's first shot went 321 yards, but he said, "No, I didn't hit that one very well. I'll try another." The mulligan went 340 yards.

Snake Situation

Playing in a tournament on an Arizona desert course, Gary Player became upset after hearing that three snakes had been killed during that day's round. He explained that snakes wouldn't bother people if they were left alone. Dave Stockton's answer was, "They won't bother you if they're dead, either."

Smoking It Out

Walter Hagen knew his approach shot had landed in a greenside bunker, but until he got there, he didn't realize it had rolled into a paper bag. He asked an official for a ruling and was told he'd either have to play it from inside the bag or take a drop and a penalty stroke. Walter had other ideas. He lit a cigarette, dropped the match onto the bag, and watched as the bag burned away. He then proceeded to get up and down for his par.

How Bubba Made the Cut

Bubba Watson was afraid he wouldn't make the cut at the Bridgestone Open, but he managed to put aside his worries and shoot his lowest round of the year to take the lead. After his round, he confessed his earlier fears to reporters, only to learn that there is no cut at the Bridgestone. Bubba just smiled and said, "Well, perfect then. I made it."

The American Calls It a Mulligan

Americans playing a round in Scotland are often impressed with how seriously the game is taken there. One Yank learned the lesson very quickly at a Scottish course. His very first drive hooked out-of-bounds, so he teed up another ball and hit it right down the middle. Turning to the caddie he said, "In America we call that a mulligan. What do you call it here?" "We call it lying three," said the caddie.

Bob Hope Vs. Gerald Ford

Comedian Bob Hope and President Gerald Ford enjoyed kidding each other on the course. Hope once jibed about Ford, "We have fifty-one golf courses in Palm Springs. He never decides which course he will play until after the first tee shot." When asked about Hope's goal of shooting his age, Ford said, "I know he'll do it someday, even if he has to live to be 125."

When Snead Visited the Vatican

Sam Snead and his manager, Fred Corcoran, were touring Europe one year. When they arrived in Rome, Corcoran arranged an audience with the Pope and encouraged Snead to bring his putter so the Pontiff could bless it. The monsignor who met them at the Vatican revealed that he was also a golfer and was having serious problems with his putting. As Snead put away his putter, he told the monsignor, "If you're a buddy of the Pope and you can't putt, he ain't gonna do anything for me."

How to Pick a Swing Coach

Lee Trevino does things the old-fashioned way:
He keeps it simple. No personal trainer, no public
relations specialist, no traveling nutritionist—just
Trevino and his caddie. When asked if he would
ever consider consulting a swing coach, Trevino
said, "When I find one who can beat me, I'll listen."

Jimmy Demaret's Crystal Ball

To Jimmy Demaret's well-known talents as a golfer
and TV analyst, add his abilities with a crystal ball.
During the 1958 Masters, Arnold Palmer had hit his
tee shot to the very back of the tricky par-3 16th
green. "There's no way he gets down in two from
back there," predicted Demaret. Palmer proceeded
to chip the ball into the hole for a birdie. "See?"
said Demaret.

Watney's 11-Stroke Hole

Nick Watney was near the top of the 2011 TPC Boston leaderboard on the final day of the tournament when he hit his ball into the water hazard just below the green on the par 5-second hole. Watney tried to chip his ball out of trouble, but it bounced off a rock—back into the hazard. In a fit of temper, he smashed his wedge against the rock: a two-stroke penalty, because the rock was in the hazard. It might take weeks or even months for Watney to watch a replay of his rock-smashing video— and appreciate the humor that made most viewers smile as they watched him toss two strokes and forty-nine positions on the leaderboard into the hazard the moment his club struck the rock.

Golfers' Fitness

There were mixed feelings about the merits of the Traveling Fitness Center when it first showed up on the PGA Tour in 1987. Gay Brewer noted, however, that it was getting a fair amount of attention. "Even Billy Casper is in there pedaling away on the bike," he said. "Of course, he rode a golf cart to get over there."

More Important Things on His Mind

After Lee Westwood finally realized his lifelong dream to become the number one golfer in the world, his father phoned to congratulate him on his top ranking. Westwood, who happened to be in a grocery store at the time, was nonchalant about the news, replying, "Yeah, yeah, yeah, hang on. I can't find the mashed potatoes."

When Trevino Is On the Road

Professional athletes travel a lot, and married ones need spouses who are considerate, sympathetic, and understanding. "My wife doesn't care what I do when I'm away," says Lee Trevino, "as long as I don't have a good time."

You've Got to Accentuate the Positive

What impressed some people about Ben Hogan was his total concentration during a match. Nothing could distract him. For example, at a Masters in the early fifties, Hogan was paired with Claude Harmon. Hogan hit first at the par-3 12th and put his shot about 10 feet from the pin. Harmon did better, putting his tee shot into the hole for an ace, and the crowd went wild. After calmly sinking his birdie putt, Hogan said, "You know, Claude, I've been waiting a long time to make a 2 on that hole."

Lyndon Johnson's Handicap

Lyndon Johnson was one of the few twentieth-century U.S. presidents who could not be accused of being a golfer. He showed up as a spectator at the Masters one year, but his motives were political. Not aware of Johnson's indifference to the game, someone at Augusta asked him what his handicap was. "Congress," said Johnson.

Choosing Words Carefully

South African golfer Simon Hobday is normally an easygoing fellow who steers clear of controversy. When he does run afoul of the rules, he chooses his words carefully. He once asked an official, "If I called you an @#!, would you fine me?" "Probably," said the official. "How about if I were just *thinking* it?" Hobday said. "No. How could I?" replied the official. "Okay, then, I *think* you're an @#! ," said Hobday.

Always the Entertainer

Alex Karras had a long, colorful football career with the Detroit Lions and was surprisingly effective as a character actor in the movies. He entertained on the golf course, too. Playing at Michigan's Red Run Golf Club, he sliced his first drive through the large window in the clubhouse dining room. Trudging over, he peered through the shattered glass and asked, "Is this room out-of-bounds?"

"Mr. Style" Rips Rickie Fowler

Rickie Fowler's rabid fans may love his wardrobe, but *Golf Digest's* "Mr. Style," Marty Hackel, thinks one of Fowler's outfits, an all-orange ensemble, is too much: "Enough already. This is like orange overload… Either move to Florida, or stop wearing all orange. Look in the mirror before you go out."

Babe's Psych-Out Tactics

Humility was not something Babe Didrikson Zaharias practiced. She was known for telling other players before the start of tournaments, "Okay, Babe's here! Now who's gonna finish second?" She also tried to psych out competitors by asking them, "Do you always hold your putter like that?"

Mutual Admiration Society

Jimmy Demaret and Ben Hogan were long-time rivals, but they admired each other greatly. Demaret was standing in a bar one night when someone told him that Hogan once said that if Jimmy were to practice more and party less, he'd win every tournament he entered. Demaret, pleased with the observation, lifted his glass and said, "I'll drink to that!"

Nicklaus's Reduced Schedule

Chi Chi Rodriguez has amassed a pretty impressive record of tournament wins. But he marvels at the incredible string of majors and other victories Jack Nicklaus has rung up. Even with his reduced schedule, Nicklaus is formidable, Chi Chi says. "Today," he adds, "he's a legend in his spare time."

Cloak and Dagger

Ben Hogan's well-known insistence on privacy extended to his work with the few pupils he took on. A writer once asked Kris Tschetter if she could discuss what Ben had helped her with. "I could tell you, of course," she said, "but then I'd have to kill you."

He Paid His Own Way

Pittsburgh sportswriter Bob Drum wanted his newspaper to send him to the British Open to cover the exploits of a hot young golfer named Arnold Palmer. His editor refused, but Drum went anyway at his own expense. To everyone's surprise, Palmer was in contention going into the final round. Drum received a wire from his editor that read, "Need a thousand words on Palmer." Drum wired back, "Hope you get it."

Irish Wit

David Feherty is well-known for his Irish wit. He tells this story about his father stumbling home after one drop too many at the pub. "Is my dinner still warm?" he asked his long-suffering wife. "Yes," she said, "it's in the dog."

Long Hitters

Browse any magazine rack and you're likely to find a golf magazine that promises instruction on how to hit the ball farther. Harvey Penick, who coached six members of the World Golf Hall of Fame including Ben Crenshaw and Tom Kite, couldn't have agreed less with the obsession for distance. He often warned his students, "The woods are full of long hitters."

Ben Hogan for President

During his two terms in the White House, Dwight Eisenhower did a lot to popularize golf. However, politics being the unsavory business it is, his detractors turned his love for the game against him during the 1956 election. They circulated a poster that read, "Ben Hogan for president. If we're going to have a golfer, let's have a good one."

Unofficial Ruling

We're indebted to one of Tommy Bolt's regular partners for this tale, although he prefers to remain anonymous. Tommy had just blown an iron shot and, in a rage, threw the offending club into the nearby lake. "You'd better throw a provisional," said our contributor. "That one's probably lost."

Chi Chi's Secret Club

Everyone knows you can carry only fourteen clubs in your bag, and everyone has his favorite go-to club. But Chi Chi Rodriguez suggests that a lot of players also have a secret club to rely upon in emergencies. For most amateurs, he says, "the best wood in the bag is the pencil."

Sam Snead Vs. Ted Williams

Two masters of their respective sports, Ted Williams and Sam Snead, were discussing the relative difficulties of their games. Williams maintained that nothing could be harder than hitting a baseball coming at you at a hundred miles an hour. "Maybe so," said Snead, "but you don't have to go into the stands and play your foul balls like we do."

Tiger Woods's Mulligan

As if Tiger Woods didn't have enough problems, his name recently topped the *Miami New Times* list of "cheapest celebrity tippers." The man who's worth more than $500 million took a mulligan on a $5 tip while playing a high-stakes game of blackjack. He put the money back into his pocket because he had already tipped the server earlier in the evening.

Nicklaus's Wake-Up Call

In his pre-tournament analysis of the 1986 Masters, *The Atlanta Journal-Constitution's* Tom McCollister wrote off Jack Nicklaus as "too old, washed up, done." After Jack shot a final-round 65 to win the green jacket, McCollister walked into the crowded interview room and heard Nicklaus say, "Thanks for the inspiration, Tom." "Glad I could help," said McCollister.

Ruling Request

Tommy Bolt was playing a round with a caddie who was getting on his nerves. Finally, after a particularly heated exchange about club selection, Bolt asked a tournament official for a ruling. "I know I can be fined for throwing a club," Bolt said, "but is there a penalty for throwing a caddie?"

The Early Days of Televised Golf

In the early sixties, golf began drawing a respectable TV audience, and televising the big-money match between Byron Nelson and Gene Littler became quite an event. With a TV camera poised about 250 yards down the first fairway, Nelson blasted a huge drive right down the middle. As Littler prepared to hit, a cameraman picked up Nelson's ball and ran it back to the tee. "Would you please hit it again, Mr. Nelson?" he asked. "We weren't ready."

"Billigans"

After playing golf with President Bill Clinton, Bryce Molder described the experience as "weird." "He shot a 90—but at the end of the game, his scorecard said 84." That's not as weird as the time Clinton took 200 swings and recorded an 82 on his scorecard—a golf outing reported by *New York Times* reporter Don Van Natta, in which he coined a memorable term for Clinton's 112 mulligans: "Billigans."

The Hollywood Drinking Champion

Singer/comedian Phil Harris held the Hollywood Drinking Championship title for quite a few years. (And that's a pretty tough league.) Once, he and Bing Crosby were golfing in Scotland, and as they drove by a Scotch distillery one evening, Crosby said, "See Phil, they're making it faster than you can drink it." "Maybe," said Harris, "but I've got 'em working nights."

When Rory McIlroy Was Nine

When Rory McIlroy was nine, he appeared on a local TV show and wore a big smile as he answered three questions: "How far can you drive a ball?" "300 yards," said McIlroy. "Do you want to be a professional golfer when you grow up?" "Yes," said McIlroy. "Who's your favorite Irish golfer?" "Darren Clarke," said McIlroy. Then Rory chipped a golf ball about 15 feet into a washing machine. McIlroy went on to become a professional golfer at the age of eighteen and win the U.S. Open when he was twenty-one—about three months before his childhood idol Darren Clarke won his first major, the British Open.

Dapper Doug

In the late eighties, as the Senior Tour was gaining popularity, the dapper Doug Sanders admitted modestly to a reporter that there were two players people invariably asked about after every tournament: himself and Arnold Palmer. "They want to know what Arnold shot and what I was wearing," explained Sanders.

Quick Study

No hole-in-one hysterics for songwriter and avid golfer Hoagy Carmichael. Teeing off on a par-3 one day, he hit a shot that took one bounce on the green, hit the pin, and dropped directly into the hole. Without skipping a beat, he pulled out another ball, teed it up, and said, "I think I've got the hang of this now."

The Editor's Ego

Bill Davis was one of the founders of *Golf Digest* and ran the magazine for many years. He was smart but quirky and unpredictable, and some of his eccentricities drove many of his writers to distraction. At his retirement dinner, he spoke of the editor's relationship with the writer. "Even Hemingway would have been a better writer if I had edited him," he bragged. "True," agreed a writer in the audience, "but he'd also have committed suicide ten years sooner."

Jim Furyk's Ugly Swing

Baseball great Ted Williams once said to upcoming star Carl Yastrzemski, "Don't ever let anyone monkey with your swing." The same advice applied to Jim Furyk's ugly but effective swing. A college coach recruiting Furyk told the young player's father he couldn't wait to get Jim to campus to "change that swing." Furyk's father Mike, who had been his son's only swing instructor, told the coach, "He'll never play for you." He never did.

Silent for 17 Holes

If a record exists for the fewest words spoken during a golf match, tight-lipped Harry Vardon probably holds it with one. In a tense match with Bobby Jones, Vardon had said nothing through 17 holes. Then, on 18, Jones skulled a fairway shot and, furious with himself, screamed, "DID YOU EVER SEE SUCH A TERRIBLE SHOT!" "No," said Vardon.

How Thick Was the Rough, Lee?

Lee Trevino is not particularly fond of British courses. After a practice round before a British Open at St. Andrews, Trevino complained about the thick rough he and his caddie plunged into near the 15th green. Someone asked if they found the ball. "Yes, we found the ball," said Trevino, "but we lost the bag."

Lowered Expectations

Tony Kornheiser of the *Washington Post* shares a goal with many amateur golfers: breaking 100 consistently. However, as he looks ahead, Tony sees little chance of reaching the goal of many senior players: shooting one's age. "I'll be lucky to shoot my body temperature," he says.

Don't Blame the Rental Clubs

After his golf clubs were lost on the way to the Czech Open, Pedro Oriol was forced to play with loaners. But don't feel too bad for him: He ended the first round one shot off the lead. Oriol was pragmatic about his up-and-down luck, saying, "I'm not sure I'm going to switch back to my own clubs now even if they arrive."

Chi Chi's Distance Off the Tee

Thanks to the Senior Tour, Chi Chi Rodriguez is making more money than ever, and his theatrics on the course are getting as many laughs as ever. One difference he's noticed, however, is his distance off the tee. "The older you get," he says, "the longer you used to be."

Lee Trevino's 1-Iron Rule

Lee Trevino is like most golfers in at least one respect: He has trouble hitting the 1-iron. So why does he carry the club? Apparently to hold straight up in the air while walking off a course as lightning threatens. "Not even God can hit a 1-iron," he explains.

Which Casper Will You Get?

You never know which Billy Casper is going to show up at the next senior tournament: the 220-pound Billy Casper (at one U.S. Open) or the 180-pound Billy Casper (at the next one). His buffalo meat diet, among others, has kept his tailors busy and happy. As ex-quarterback John Brody put it, "Billy Casper has won more titles at more different weights than Sugar Ray Leonard."

The "King of Aces"

Known as the "King of Aces," Mancil Davis has made fifty-one holes-in-one. Is he impressed by this fact? Heck no. In fact, he echoed the sentiments of many golfers when he said, "It is pretty hard to believe that I have more [holes-in-one] than the great ball strikers that have played this crazy game, but believe me, I would trade all of those 'ones' for Tiger's swing!"

Word Origin

Variations on the word *golf* go back to the beginning of the game itself, but no one can pin down its exact origin or what the word meant. Writer George Peper has a theory: "According to locker-room lore, the name *golf* arose by default," he says. "All the other four-letter words had already been taken."

Paul Harvey Gets His Wish

One of the few black days in the golfing life of Jack Nicklaus was the opening round of the 1987 British Open. Nothing went right that day, and Jack carded a miserable 83. Not everyone was unhappy though. Broadcaster Paul Harvey was overheard in the gallery saying, "All my life I've wanted to play like Jack Nicklaus...and now I can!"

How Bad Were the Fairways?

Who said it's easy to run a golf course? Doug Thompson, general manager of the Hyland Golf Club in Southern Pines, had to watch his course go without irrigation for twenty-six days due to a system failure. "Our fairways were awful," he said. "They looked like Fort Bragg had messed up its firing range coordinates."

O.J. Simpson's Punishment

People were upset when O.J. Simpson walked away a free man. Leave it to comedian George Carlin to put it in perspective: "O.J. Simpson has already received the ultimate punishment. For the rest of his life, he has to associate with golfers."

Married-Couple Competition

When it came to married-couple competition, few could compete with Judy and Gardner Dickinson. There was a time, however, when Judy was riding high on the LPGA Tour and Gardner wasn't doing too well in PGA play. Apparently, their relationship wasn't doing too well either. During one of their domestic spats, Judy took a cheap shot: "Oh God, Gardner," she said, "sometimes I think you married me just to see your name on the leaderboard."

The Ultimate Test

Robert Trent Jones was taking a lot of heat for his 1954 U.S. Open redesign of the par-3 fourth hole at Baltusrol. So he and a few committee members walked out to the tee box at 4, where Jones dropped a ball and hit it...right into the cup. He turned to the group and said, "The hole certainly seems fair to me."

"Rickie Fowler Runs Over His Driver"

When that headline found its way online, shocked readers thought, "OH MY GOD! Rickie Fowler ran over his chauffeur." But when they read the rest of the story, they discovered that Fowler had accidentally backed his car over his golf bag and bent his driver out of shape. Poor guy; his agent had to call the golf-club manufacturer and ask for a free replacement.

Alan Shepard's Moon Shot

Unbeknownst to NASA, astronaut Alan Shepard smuggled the blade from a 6-iron and two golf balls into his spacesuit before blasting off for the moon in 1971. Once he landed, Shepard attached the club-head to a rock-and-soil sampling tool with a barrel grip and a cylindrical shaft, removed one golf ball from his suit, and announced to a live TV audience, "I'm going to try a sand-trap shot here." His first swing whiffed. His second swing barely moved the ball. He shanked his third shot. But his fourth swing knocked it stiff—sending the ball 300 yards through space. In that semi-historic moment, Shepard hit the moon shot seen 'round the world.

One Way to Win a Bet

Chi Chi Rodriguez is best known for his humorous antics on the golf course. Once, while playing a Nassau at a course in Puerto Rico, he closed out his opponent on the 17th hole and then offered him an attractive press on 18. "I'll give you two strokes and you give me one throw for all the marbles," said Rodriguez. They agreed, and both reached the par-4 green in two, with Rodriguez away. "I think I'll take my throw now," said Rodriguez. And with that he picked up his opponent's ball and tossed it far out into the ocean. "With your drop, you're now lying four," said Rodriguez. "And you're away."

A Weather Prediction That's All Wet

Larry David, creator and star of the TV show *Curb Your Enthusiasm*, is a big golf fan who plays in several charity events a year. His enthusiasm has also made it onto his show. In one scene, his character wonders aloud, "What if the weatherman predicts it's going to rain just so he can keep people off the golf course so he can have it for himself?"

The Whole Truth

Not telling the whole truth can get a guy in trouble. Sam Snead was standing on the 16th fairway at Firestone, consulting his caddie about his shot. "Jay Hebert hit an 8-iron from here yesterday," the caddie said. So Sam pulled out his 8-iron and hit the ball right into the lake guarding the green. "Where did Hebert hit his 8-iron yesterday?" asked Snead. "Into the lake," said the caddie.

Evel Knievel's Golf Cart Jump

Famous daredevil Evel Knievel learned the hard way to be wary of golf carts. Here's his story: "In the mid-seventies, I played a lot of golf at Rivermont in Alpharetta, Georgia. The 17th hole there is a par 3 that's steeply downhill. The path has a series of hairpin turns, and if you ignore them you'll just keep going over a huge ledge. The guys I hung out with pointed out that if you gathered enough speed you could go over the cliff and land where the path resumes farther down the hill. For days they dared me to make the jump, and when I came to the hole in a foul mood one afternoon— I wasn't playing well—I just went for it. Halfway down the hill I realized I'd made a mistake. You have no idea how unstable a three-wheel golf cart is when it becomes airborne. By the grace of God I made a perfect three-point landing, but the tires were like basketballs, and the cart bounced like a #@%! When I got the thing stopped down near the green, I immediately got a royal chewing out from my wife. I couldn't blame her. She'd been in the passenger seat the whole time."

Smoker's Blues

When South African golfer Fulton Allem first came to the United States to try his luck on the pro tour, he was troubled by the aversion to smoking in this country. "I was familiar with the old slogan, 'I'd walk a mile for a Camel,'" Allem said, "but now it seems you have to walk a mile to smoke one."

Supersized Sand Trap

The new Ocean Trails course in Rancho Palos Verdes suffered a bit of a setback in June of 1999 when the 18th hole slid down a bluff toward the Pacific Ocean. Writer Jerry Perisho tried to look on the bright side. "Sure, the 18th fairway now has a twenty-six-thousand acre sand trap and a water hazard that stretches all the way to Japan," he said, "but now everyone gets to hit from the ladies' tee."

Lee and Chi Chi Go Fishing

Lee Trevino and Chi Chi Rodriguez were in Minnesota just before the 1970 U.S. Open at Hazeltine, and they decided to rent a boat and do a little fishing on one of the state's ten thousand lakes. They found a great spot and hauled in a huge catch of largemouth bass. As the sun started to set and they prepared to head back in, Rodriguez suggested that Trevino mark the lucky spot in case they had a chance to come back. Upon reaching the dock, Rodriguez asked Trevino how he had marked the place. "Right here on the side of the boat," said Trevino. "That's no good!" said Rodriguez. "What if we don't get the same boat?"

Scottish Reserve

At the 1975 British Open at Carnoustie, Jack Nicklaus and Tom Watson were shooting an evening practice round when they got a taste of flinty Scottish reserve. On a difficult par-3, with the green tucked behind some mounds, they both hit good tee shots but weren't sure how they turned out. Upon reaching the green, they saw Nicklaus's ball and eventually found Watson's...in the hole. Marveling at the lack of excitement from the small gallery, Nicklaus approached two elderly gentlemen and asked if they saw Watson's ball go in. "Aye," said one of the men, "but it's only practice, isn't it?"

Not Everyone Recognizes Arnold Palmer

Just because Arnold Palmer is probably the best-recognized golfer of all time doesn't mean *everyone* knows him. Palmer once did a TV commercial that required him to hit shots onto a green. As Arnie hit ball after ball at the flag, one of the camera crew was so impressed that he commented to a fellow worker, "This guy is wasting his time being an actor. He could be a pro golfer!"

Stuck in a Bunker

In the 1990 PGA Seniors tournament, Jack Nicklaus found himself with a very difficult bunker shot. After a couple of unsuccessful attempts to extricate himself, Jack was fuming. "Who designed this #*+! bunker?" he moaned. His rage turned to sheepishness, however, when an official pointed out that he, Nicklaus, had designed the course.

The Best Golf Psychiatrist

Old-timer Jackie Burke thinks that with swing coaches and mental coaches and the like, the modern golf game has become too complicated. "Jimmy Demaret and I had the best golf psychiatrist in the world," he says. "His name was Jack Daniels, and he was waiting for us after every round."

Feherty's Divorce Diet

Before David Feherty became a TV analyst, he was a moderately successful touring pro. But in 1995, his game and his marriage fell apart at about the same time. Before finally getting straightened out, he dealt with his problems in two ways, both a bit extreme. He went on what he calls his divorce diet (coffee, cigarettes, Advil, and alcohol), and he started running a hundred miles a week. The net result? "I lost 40 pounds," he says. "150 if you include my wife."

The Turning Point

In the 1946 PGA Championship at the Portland Golf Club, Ben Hogan thrashed Jimmy Demaret in the finals, ending the match up 10 and 9. A reporter asked the humbled Demaret if there had been a turning point in the match. "Yes," said Jimmy, "when Ben showed up."

Two Sharks

The golfing careers of Greg Norman and Chi Chi Rodriguez peaked at different times, but Rodriguez has noticed similarities between the two players. For example, both are referred to as sharks. "Norman's known as the White Shark," explains Rodriguez, "and among my associates, I'm known as the Loan Shark."

A Typo or the Truth?

This is, perhaps, a semi-Freudian slip. A North Carolina tourist brochure reads, "Famous mid-South resorts, including Pinehurst and Southern Pines, have more golf curses per mile than anywhere else in the world."

Ben Hogan, Golf Course Critic

Ben Hogan had something in common with a lot of pro golfers. He disliked many of the courses designed or remodeled by architect Robert Trent Jones. Hogan thought they were too tough and was not reluctant to criticize Jones's work openly. After being congratulated by Trent's wife, Ione, at the end of a tournament on one of Jones's courses, Hogan coolly responded, "If your husband had to play his courses for a living, you'd both be on the breadline."

The Voice from the Porta-potty

Jim Ferree found himself in a delicate situation during the 1960 World Series of Golf at the Firestone Country Club. He had overshot the fourth green and his ball came to rest next to a porta-potty. As he prepared to hit his approach, an official advised Ferree to wait because someone seemed to be in the facility. If the occupant emerged during Ferree's backswing, it would be a distraction. As everyone stood and stared at the outhouse, a muffled voice from inside called out, "Go ahead and hit!"

Practice Didn't Make Justin Perfect

Singer Justin Timberlake is so obsessed with improving his golf game, he built a five-hole outdoor course at his Los Angeles mansion; he practices inside by using bundled blankets for sand traps and overturned couches and tables for hazards. There's one person he won't play, though: his girlfriend, actress Jessica Biel. After she took up the game, she beat him on his own course.

If You Putt Too Slowly...

Although Ben Hogan was a formidable and intimidating figure, Chris Dunphy was one of the few in golf who stood up to him. Dunphy was the president at Seminole, a course Hogan liked to play when preparing for the Masters. In his later years, Hogan spent more time preparing to putt, and during a round they played together, Hogan complained about the Seminole greens being too slow. "If you didn't take so long to putt," replied Dunphy, "the grass wouldn't be so long."

Fashion Imitates Life

You've heard that art imitates life, but according to comedian Buddy Hackett, so does fashion. "Once, playing in Georgia, I hooked a ball through some woods and into a swamp," he said. "When I went in to look for it, I found an alligator wearing a shirt with a little golfer on it."

Ryder Cup Jitters

Even though no big-bucks prize money is involved, there's something about Ryder Cup competition that produces emotions and tensions even the majors can't rival. Veteran José María Olazábal put it nicely when he described approaching the first shot in Ryder Cup competition: "Everything shakes except the shaft of your club," he said, "and that's because it's still in the bag."

Bobby Jones's Honesty

In the second round of the 1925 U.S. Open, Bobby Jones was in danger of missing the cut. On the 11th hole, he pushed a shot into the rough to the right of the green. From there he had apparently lobbed onto the green, but then he announced that his ball had moved in the rough as he first addressed it, and he declared a penalty on himself. He was highly praised for his honesty, but he would have none of it. "That's nonsense," said Jones. "You might as well praise me for not robbing a bank!"

Sticks and Stones

During the 1991 Ryder Cup matches, Paul Azinger caused a big flap by calling NBC analyst Johnny Miller "the biggest moron I've ever seen in the booth." As the controversy grew, Azinger protested that he had been misquoted. What did he claim to have said? "I called him the biggest Mormon I'd ever seen in the booth."

Murphy's Metaphors

Sports announcers come in all shapes, sizes, and styles. For example, Vin Scully was Mr. Smooth when announcing the action, whereas Dizzy Dean mangled the language. But few could match the sheer poetry of golf announcer Bob Murphy. When describing a delicate approach shot by Lee Trevino back in 1989, Murphy observed, "It came in there like a butterfly with sore feet."

The Right Caddie for the Job

After a long, lonely search, singer/comedian Phil Harris finally found the right caddie: one who drank as well (or at least as much) as he did. Their relationship was strained, however, when one day they both showed up at the first tee in terrible shape. Harris, after some difficulty getting his ball teed up, took a wild and tortured swing at it. "Where did it go?" asked Harris. "Where did what go?" the caddie responded.

Hanging Out with Celebrities

Show biz celebrities love to play in the Pro-Ams where they can hang around the big hitters on the tour. But what about the pros? Do they like to rub elbows with the stars of stage and screen? Jimmy Demaret didn't seem too impressed a few years back: "Two of my favorite celebrities are comedian Bing Crosby and singer Bob Hope. Or is it the other way around? I always forget which one thinks he's funny and which one thinks he can sing."

When Golfers Retire

What are you going to do when you retire? Most people of the male persuasion respond, "Fish and golf." But among those who find fault with both the question and the answer is long-time pro Julius Boros. When asked late in his career if that were his plan, Julius said, "Why would I want to retire at all? All I do now is fish and golf."

Lee Trevino, Window Cleaner

Sounds like Lee Trevino's bank account is so fat he's turning down opportunities to make a few bucks on the side. Lee was washing the front windows of his home in Dallas one day when a car pulled into his driveway. A woman got out and asked him what he charged for that service. "It depends," he said. "At this house, the lady lets me sleep with her."

Chi Chi's Accent

Chi Chi Rodriguez's Puerto Rican accent has caused some funny mishaps throughout his career. "After all these years, it's still embarrassing for me to play on the American golf tour," he joked. "Like the time I asked my caddie for a sand wedge and he came back ten minutes later with a ham on rye."

Why They Failed

In 1992, members of the Boston Amateur Golf Society launched an earnest campaign to increase membership in their Women's Section. When they did not meet with much success, someone pointed out that it might have something to do with their logo and the Society's acronym: BAGS.

Keeping Quiet

Many pro golfers are associated with their individual characteristics. Lee Trevino is glib, Arnold Palmer is flamboyant, Ben Hogan was tight-lipped. How about Tom Lehman? Well, according to Justin Leonard, the description for Tom is "straight arrow." After playing a round with Lehman, Leonard said, "We didn't speak for fifteen holes because I couldn't think of a clean joke to tell him."

Palmer Gets Even

You've heard the advice, "Don't get mad, get even!"
Well, it took a while, but Arnold Palmer got even. He
grew up on the Latrobe Country Club golf course
near Pittsburgh, where his father, Deacon, was the
club pro. But being an employee's child, Arnie was
denied certain member privileges like playing in club
tournaments and swimming in the pool. What did
he do about it? Years later, after he became rich and
famous, Palmer came home and bought the club.

Slow-Play Disease

The curse of the public golf course is slow play—
the six-hour round. But even a few pros suffer from
slow-play disease. Like Bernhard Langer, according to
some. He and Lee Trevino were paired for a round in
1992, and as Trevino was coming off the 18th green,
he was asked to comment on Langer's new beard:
"He was clean-shaven when we teed off."

Index

Aaron, Hank, 14
Allem, Fulton, 71
Azinger, Paul, 32, 79

Babineau, Jeff, 41
Baddeley, Aaron, 35
Ballesteros, Seve, 30
Beard, Frank, 7
Beman, Deane, 16
Biel, Jessica, 77
Bolt, Tommy, 12, 23, 26, 32, 35, 54, 55
Boros, Julius, 80
Boswell, Charlie, 11
Brewer, Gay, 30, 47
Brody, John, 63
Buckner, Bill, 27
Burke, Jackie, 15, 73
Bush, Barbara, 35
Bush, George, 35

Caponi, Donna, 4
Carlin, George, 66
Carmichael, Hoagy, 59
Casper, Billy, 47, 63
Clarke, Darren, 58
Clinton, Bill, 35, 57
Cole, Bobby, 33
Corcoran, Fred, 45
Costas, Bob, 23
Crenshaw, Ben, 28, 36, 53
Crosby, Bing, 57, 80

Daly, John, 11, 30, 42
David, Larry, 69
Davis, Bill, 59
Davis, Mancil, 64

Dean, Dizzy, 79
DeGeneres, Ellen, 6
Demaret, Jimmy, 2, 4, 23, 40, 42, 46, 51, 73, 74, 80
Dent, Jim, 11, 42
Dickinson, Gardner, 66
Dickinson, Judy, 66
Douglas, Michael, 24
Drum, Bob, 52
Dunphy, Chris, 13, 77
Durante, Jimmy, 6

Eisenhower, Dwight, 53
Els, Ernie, 39

Faldo, Nick, 18
Faxon, Brad, 5
Feherty, David, 2, 17, 22, 53, 74
Feherty, William, 17
Ferree, Jim, 76
Ford, Gerald, 35, 44
Fowler, Rickie, 51, 67
Furyk, Jim, 60

Gallico, Paul, 14
Geiberger, Al, 12
Geiberger, Brent, 12
Gleason, Jackie, 29
Goldwyn, Sam, 12
Goydos, Paul, 23
Graham, Billy, 20

Hackel, Marty, 51
Hackett, Buddy, 77
Hagen, Walter, 22, 32, 43
Harmon, Claude, 19, 48
Harmon, Dick, 19

Harris, Phil, 57, 79
Harvey, Paul, 65
Hebert, Jay, 69
Hobday, Simon, 49
Hogan, Ben, 2, 9, 26, 41, 48, 51,
    52, 53, 74, 75, 77, 82
Holland, Trey, 39
Hope, Bob, 5, 9, 12, 44, 80

Jenkins, Dan, 28
Johnson, Elaine, 9
Johnson, Lyndon, 49
Jones, Bobby, 60, 78
Jones, Robert Trent, 4, 66, 75
Jordan, Michael, 10

Karras, Alex, 50
Kennedy, John F., 13
Kerr, Cristie, 34
Kim, Christina, 26
Kite, Tom, 53
Knievel, Evel, 70
Kornheiser, Tony, 62

Langer, Bernhard, 83
Lehman, Melissa, 31
Lehman, Tom, 31, 82
Lema, Tony, 37
Lemmon, Jack, 24
Leonard, Justin, 82
Lewis, Joe E., 24
Littler, Gene, 18, 31, 56

MacDonald, Fiona, 38
Maltbie, Roger, 34
Martin, Dean, 24
Mazzeo, Mike, 14, 37
McCollister, Tom, 55
McIlroy, Rory, 58

Mickelson, Phil, 13, 41
Middlecoff, Cary, 28
Miller, Johnny, 79
Molder, Bryce, 57
Murphy, Bob, 79
Murray, Jim, 4, 7, 9

Na, Kevin, 8
Natta, Don Van, 57
Nelson, Byron, 15, 42, 56
Nelson, Willie, 20
Nicklaus, Jack, 7, 16, 24, 32, 36,
    52, 55, 65, 72, 73
Norman, Greg, 42, 74

Obama, Barack, 20
Olazábal, José María, 78
Oriol, Pedro, 62

Palmer, Arnold, 5, 9, 18, 27, 31,
    40, 46, 52, 58, 73, 82, 83
Parnevik, Jesper, 28
Patton, Billy Joe, 39
Penick, Harvey, 28, 53
Peper, George, 64
Perisho, Jerry, 71
Player, Gary, 32, 43
Pride, Dicky, 4

Quayle, Dan, 8
Quayle, Marilyn, 8

Rodriguez, Chi Chi, 32, 52, 54,
    62, 68, 72, 74, 82
Russell, Bill, 19

Sanders, Doug, 27, 58
Scott, Ray, 2
Scully, Vin, 79

Shepard, Alan, 67
Simpson, O.J., 66
Snead, Sam, 21, 33, 45, 54, 69
Stadler, Craig, 26
Stenson, Henrik, 16
Stockton, Dave, 43

Taylor, Dick, 16
Thompson, Doug, 65
Timberlake, Justin, 77
Tomlin, Lily, 18
Trevino, Lee, 11, 20, 25, 34, 37,
    46, 48, 61, 63, 72, 79, 81,
    82, 83
Truman, Harry, 20
Tschetter, Kris, 52

Vardon, Harry, 60
Venturi, Ken, 7, 40
Verdi, Bob, 30

Wadkins, Lanny, 19
Watney, Nick, 47
Watson, Bubba, 6, 44
Watson, Tom, 72
Westwood, Lee, 13, 48
Whitaker, Jack, 7
Williams, Ted, 54, 60
Woods, Tiger, 5, 10, 11, 32, 35, 55

Yastrzemski, Carl, 60
Yokomine, Sakura, 26

Zaharias, Babe Didrikson, 14, 51
Zoeller, Fuzzy, 14, 30, 37